The Sounds Around Us

Matthew Gose

Rosen
REAL
READERS

Rosen Classroom Books & Materials
New York

The bell rings.

The clock ticks.

The people talk.

The cat meows.

The rain taps on the car.

The radio plays music.

Words to Know

car

clock

radio

rain